3/01

Digging for Bird-Dinosaurs

An Expedition to Madagascar

Nic Bishop

Houghton Mifflin Company Boston 2000

For Cathy and all others who have found their passion and not let go

Copyright © 2000 by Nic Bishop
Map and diagram copyright © 2000 by Houghton Mifflin Company

The text of this book is set in 12-point Rotis Serif.
Map (p. 11) and diagram (p. 45) by Jerry Malone

Library of Congress Cataloging-in-Publication Data

Bishop, Nic.
Digging for bird-dinosaurs : an expedition to Madagascar / Nic Bishop.
p.   cm.
Summary: The story of Cathy Forster's experiences as a member of a team of paleontologists
who went on an expedition to the island of Madagascar in 1998 to search for fossil birds.
ISBN 0-395-96056-8
1. Dinosaurs — Madagascar — Juvenile literature. 2. Birds, Fossil — Madagascar — Juvenile literature.
3. Forster, Cathy — Journeys — Madagascar. [1. Dinosaurs — Madagascar. 2. Birds, Fossil — Madagascar.
3. Forster, Cathy. 4. Madagascar.]   I. Title.
QE862.D5B525   2000
567.9'09691 — dc21
99-36145
CIP

Printed in Hong Kong
SCP 10 9 8 7 6 5 4 3 2 1

The Mystery of Bird-Dinosaurs

Cathy Forster was three years old when she first discovered dinosaurs. It was Christmas Day. As she opened one of her presents, out fell six of the strangest toy animals she had ever seen. Cathy was hooked even before her dad explained what they were.

Now, as a paleontologist at the State University of New York at Stony Brook, discovering dinosaurs is Cathy's job. Her lab is filled with fossils from expeditions all over the world. The benches are covered with tyrannosaur teeth found in Montana, dinosaur skulls excavated in Madagascar, an iguanodontian from South Africa, and crocodile

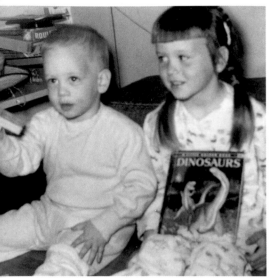

Above: Cathy was fascinated by dinosaurs as a girl.

Opposite: Cathy picks out two primitive bird-dinosaur bones from a drawer in her lab.

bones from Zimbabwe. Hundreds of other fossil bones are catalogued and carefully stored on shelves or in the cabinets that line the walls.

Cathy has loved to explore the outdoors and collect things ever since she was a little girl growing up in West St. Paul, Minnesota. On weekends and after school she would head to Mud Lake with her best friend, Nan. Together they climbed trees, caught turtles, or looked for snakes. "I filled my bedroom with things I found on my adventures," she recalls. "I had a butterfly collection, a shell collection, and a rock collection."

Whenever she had a chance, Cathy also collected fossils. "They were mostly fossil shells— the sorts of things any young collector finds," she says. "My dad had studied biology in college, so he was always very patient with my interest in nature. It was just as well, since I often pestered my parents to take me to the science museum at St. Paul to see the dinosaurs. I loved to look at them all, but my favorite was a *Triceratops,* with three horns on its head. It was fabulous."

Much later, Cathy studied *Triceratops* for her doctoral degree at the University of Pennsylvania. Then after several years her curiosity turned toward other dinosaurs. Since coming to the State University of New York in 1994, Cathy has studied one of the greatest dinosaur mysteries of all: the evolution of birds.

People are fascinated by birds. We marvel at the magic of their flight and the extraordinary details of their wings and feathers. Birds are so different from other animals, it's natural to wonder how they evolved. What did their ancestors look like? What events led to the evolution of flight?

"We still don't know the answers to all these questions," Cathy says. "The biggest problem is that bird fossils are very rare. Their bones are so fine and fragile they tend to get broken up before they turn into fossils." As Cathy talks, she opens a special drawer in her lab. Inside are rows of small boxes filled with bones, some no larger than matchsticks. She picks out two bones and holds them gently, as if they were antique china. "These come from a very primitive bird that lived alongside the dinosaurs about 70 million years ago. We discovered it in Madagascar, and it's new to science."

Cathy believes that birds are closely related to dinosaurs. "If you study a modern bird skeleton you can find many things that are similar to dinosaurs," she says. "And if you look at primitive bird bones like these, it can be hard to tell them apart from dinosaur bones."

Many scientists go so far as to say that birds are a type of dinosaur. If this is true, then dinosaurs are not really extinct after all. Even though *Tyrannosaurus, Triceratops,* and most other dinosaurs died out, one group survived—the birds. This idea sounds unbelievable at first. Do we really have feathered dinosaurs flying around the garden? But it does make some sense. Birds have scaly feet like dinosaurs, with three forward-pointing clawed toes and a hallux, a big toe that points backward. They lay eggs as dinosaurs do and, like some dinosaurs, they run on two legs.

Paleontologists first wondered about the link between birds and dinosaurs more than a hundred years ago. In the mid-nineteenth century some strange fossil animals were discovered in a limestone quarry in Germany. They had feathers like birds, but unlike any bird we know, their beaks had teeth and their wings had sharp claws. They also had the long bony tail of a reptile. They looked as much like dinosaurs as like birds. These creatures were named *Archaeopteryx,* from Greek

words meaning "ancient wing," and they were hailed as one of the most important scientific discoveries ever made. Scientists who studied *Archaeopteryx* started to think that birds must have evolved from dinosaurs.

But not everyone agreed. One paleontologist pointed out that one of *Archaeopteryx*'s bones, called the collarbone or wishbone, was not found among dinosaurs, so they could not be related. In time, scientists began to believe that birds were not descended from dinosaurs after all but from some other reptile group that lived a lot earlier.

"In the end," says Cathy, "there really wasn't enough evidence to say one way or the other, and for a very long time no more fossil birds were found." Not only are fossil bird bones rare, but fossil impressions showing that an animal had feathers are even rarer. Yet without some feather impressions, it can be hard to recognize a fossil bird. For a long time, even museum experts mistook some *Archaeopteryx* specimens for dinosaurs because they lacked clear feather impressions.

But in the last twenty years, new evidence has come to light. Some dinosaurs have been discovered that have wishbones like birds. In China, paleontologists have made exciting finds of animals that appear to be feathered dinosaurs. One of Cathy's friends, Fernando Novas, found a two-legged dinosaur with birdlike limbs in Argentina. He called it *Unenlagia,* from a South American Indian word meaning "half-bird."

Each new discovery strengthens the argument that birds evolved from dinosaurs. But not all scientists are convinced yet. The only way to find the answer is to keep searching for evidence. That's why the two tiny bird bones Cathy holds in her hands are so important. They are small clues in the huge puzzle of bird evolution. As she puts the bones back and closes the drawer, Cathy's thoughts turn to the future. In a few weeks she will be on the hunt for fossils again, as part of a dinosaur expedition to the island of Madagascar, in the Indian Ocean.

Opposite: The skeleton of a modern-day bird, a penguin, looks on as Cathy examines fossils from a theropod, a type of dinosaur which paleontologists believe is related to birds. *Below:* This 70-million-year-old fossil bird bone (left hand) looks similar to the same type of bone from a modern-day bird.

Digging for Clues

It's 1 P.M., and the sun burns down on a small group of paleontologists working in a quarry. This is their fourth week in Mahajanga, a remote region in the northwestern part of Madagascar. It has not rained for months, and the yellow grasses that cover the surrounding hills are withered. The landscape offers little shade, especially in the quarry, where the paleontologists are feeling the 100-degree heat.

But despite the discomfort, Cathy cannot think of anywhere she'd rather be. She hunches over, shielding her face from the sun, and digs at the rock with her awl. It is very soft sandstone, so the point of the awl easily sinks into it. Sometimes she needs a hammer, but often she can simply dig with the awl by hand. Like the other paleontologists, Cathy works methodically, loosening fragments of crumbling rock and shoveling them onto the growing mound of spoils at the quarry margin.

Suddenly she feels a resistance as her awl hits something hard that's buried underneath. The feeling sends a tingle down her spine: for the second time that day she has hit dinosaur. Slowly and gently, she scrapes away at the sandstone till she sees the telltale pink-brown of a fossil bone. Next she picks up a brush to whisk away loose sand. Then she uses the awl again to loosen more of the surrounding rock. Even though she is eager to see what she has found, Cathy does not hurry. The fossil is brittle and will crumble with careless digging.

She hopes it will be a bird fossil, although that's unlikely. She would be lucky to make two or three such discoveries in her whole life. Bit by bit she awls and brushes away the sandstone. As the bone reveals itself, she squirts it with resin from a squeeze-bottle. The resin acts like glue, seeping into the porous bone and hardening it so it's less brittle.

"It looks like we've got another vertebra from that theropod dinosaur," Cathy eventually calls out. Just three feet away, two Malagasy paleontology students, Laurent and Lydia, have already exposed some rib and leg bones that probably belong to the same creature. Although it's not a bird, she is still pleased to find several pieces of the dinosaur. The more bones they have, the better they can reconstruct which theropod it is. Besides, Cathy has a special interest in

Opposite: The quarry in Madagascar. *Above:* Lydia unearths part of a theropod dinosaur's rib bone.

9

Right: Laurent carefully uses his awl and hammer to chip away the sandstone around a theropod dinosaur bone. *Below:* Then he uses a brush to remove loose sand.

theropods, since this is the group of dinosaurs most closely related to birds.

Theropods were agile, meat-eating dinosaurs that ran on their hind legs. *Tyrannosaurus* was a theropod, and so was *Velociraptor*, made famous in the movie *Jurassic Park*. Although they did not have wings, they shared many characteristics with birds. For instance, they ran on two legs and their feet were very similar to those of birds. Some theropods had hollow birdlike bones and unusual wrist joints that allowed their hands to fold in the special way a bird wing does. Some theropods also had a wishbone and a sternum, or breastbone, to which wing muscles attach in birds. In fact, scientists can list more than 100 features shared only by birds and theropod dinosaurs—so many that birds might be considered flying theropods.

What's really interesting, though, is this: if birds are so much like theropods, it's probably true that theropods were like birds in many ways as well. For example, theropods may have been warm-blooded and so every bit as active and fast-moving as birds. They probably had good eyesight and may have seen colors.

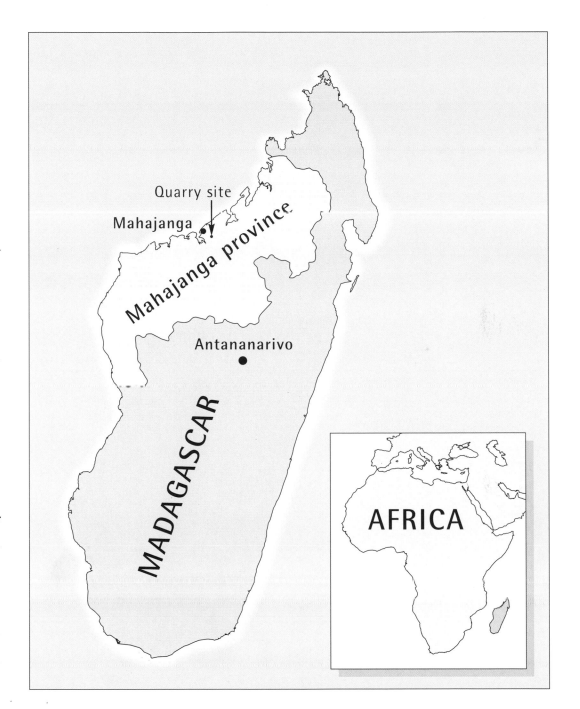

Scientists now also believe that some theropod dinosaurs made nests. In Mongolia, a fossil theropod called an *Oviraptor* was found sitting on its eggs, protecting and warming them just as an ostrich might. Although the evidence is not strong, some dinosaur parents may have brought food to the nest to feed their young, caring for them for several weeks till they were old enough to fend for themselves. Another fascinating possibility is that dinosaurs made migrations. Just as birds fly south for the winter, perhaps they made long seasonal journeys to and from their feeding and nesting areas. Some paleontologists have suggested this, but nobody really knows.

"There is so much about dinosaurs that we don't know yet," Cathy says, "but it is likely that many theropods were quick and cunning predators. They would need to be to catch their prey. Which means that the animal we are digging up here would have been a formidable creature. I wouldn't like to have met it in the flesh."

It's terrifying to contemplate a dinosaur that could pounce on its prey with the speed of a roadrunner. But might theropod dinosaurs also have had feathers like birds? A fluffy *Tyrannosaurus* is hard to imagine, but small, feathered theropods have recently been discovered in China. These creatures could not fly, so they probably had feathers for warmth, the same way that mammals have fur. The feathers also may have been brightly colored to attract mates. It was only later, when some theropods evolved winglike arms, that these feathers found another purpose—flight.

Cathy sits back and surveys her work. Two vertebrae lie at her feet, exposed to the first sunlight in 70 million years. She has uncovered only the top of each one. She won't dig these fossils out any more or lift them because they are too fragile to be handled safely. That will happen later, after they have been encased in a protective jacket of plaster. Besides, the afternoon sun is slipping toward the west, and Dave Krause, the expedition leader, announces "home time." The group packs up the tools and heads for camp.

Dinner by Starlight

Sitting in the back of the pickup truck, Cathy welcomes the breeze after a hot day at the quarry. The road to camp winds between hillsides sprinkled with neat gardens of manioc, peanuts, and papaya. Clusters of thatch huts on the ridgetops glow in the sunset. Small girls wave from open doorways and call out *"Salàma,"* which means "Hello."

As the truck turns in to camp, a group of children erupts from the grass and chases behind, running barefoot in the warm sand and laughing. They have come to play soccer with Josh and Pat, two university students who have joined the expedition. Other team members head for the tents which lie scattered across the hillside like bright candy

14

thrown into a field of hay. After cleaning up a bit and writing field notes of the day's discoveries, everyone gathers near the mess tent, where the food is kept and where Marie is busy cooking dinner over a charcoal fire.

Camp life is not comfortable. Dinner is the same most nights—rice and beans. There's no television, no phone to call home from, no refrigerator to open for a cold drink. There's no hot shower, not even any piped water at all! All the supplies, including the food and water, have to be trucked in from the small city of Mahajanga, thirty miles away. Then there is the dust. The camp is at a place called Berivotra, meaning "big wind," and the wind blows grit into everything—sleeping bags, boots, clothes, food, even toothbrushes.

But any adventure has difficulties, and there are compensations. As daylight drains away, the inky black sky fills with countless stars, so bright you can almost read by the light. The team sits outside for dinner, enjoying the warm night air and the easy companionship of like-minded friends. They discuss the day's events and what they hope to do next. Pat talks excitedly about a birdlike bone he found in another quarry. Scott is hoping to find the skull of the theropod they were digging that day. Each of the team members, who are from several different universities and museums, studies a particular type of fossil animal—crocodile, shark, bird, or dinosaur.

After dinner, stories are swapped of other expeditions to remote places and of exciting fossil discoveries. Then Dave tells how he first came to Berivotra. He explains that a French soldier found the first fragments of dinosaur bone in this area in 1895. "He sent them back to France, to the famous paleontologist Charles Depéret, who wrote about the discovery in

15

a scientific report. I read Depéret's old report and, since Madagascar has always fascinated me because of all the bizarre animals that live here today, I decided then and there to mount an expedition. I knew that if there were a few fragments, there would be more bones to find. So we flew over in 1993. It was a big adventure: we never knew what we would find. But we needn't have worried; there were bones everywhere, and we picked up our first really important fossil—a tooth from an ancient mammal—within twenty minutes!"

"On that first trip I remember asking one of the village leaders, named Retsieva, for permission to camp on their land. Even though we were complete strangers, the people welcomed us and have been good to us from that day on. Really, the success of our expeditions is due to their kindness and hospitality."

Dave's voice turns thoughtful as he continues. "The people who live here

have most of the things they need. They grow their own food, build their own houses, and have a caring community. But they do have one big worry."

Earlier that day, he had talked with some parents from the village, who were troubled that their children had no school. Dave is worried too. "The problem is that these people are too isolated for the government to build them a school. They have started to build their own but have no money for books and materials, or for a teacher. They have no way to earn money so far from the city." Dave asks the others what they think about starting a charity to help the people with their school.

That night as she writes in her diary, Cathy also wonders about the children, many of whom she knows by name. She thinks of her own childhood and the freedom that education gave her to follow her dreams of studying dinosaurs. Shouldn't these kids have that same freedom?

Opposite: Children from Berivotra chase after the pickup truck as it enters the camp. *Left:* The tents lit at night. *Below:* Supplies from the mess tent.

19

A Discovery?

"Hey Cathy!" Dave yells at the quarry. "Come check this out. I think I've got something you'll be interested in." Poking out of the rock that Dave has been digging is a small hollow bone. "You could be right," Cathy says, taking a close look. "It looks like bird."

Cathy crouches over the bone and delicately begins exposing it. She falls silent, hoping that this is the discovery she wants. What kind of bird is it? How big a bird is it? The questions race through her mind as she works, but she keeps her excitement in check. After all, this could be a small theropod dinosaur bone. They can look so similar.

The bone appears to be brittle as she digs. A tiny chip falls off, and she worries about damaging other small bones from the same animal that might be hidden in the surrounding sandstone. Finally she decides to excavate the fossil and its surrounding rock in one large block. That way everything can be transported safely home and worked on in the university lab. Even though she's bursting with curiosity, it's better to be patient. After all, the bones have waited 70 million years. A few more months won't hurt.

All around Cathy, the quarry is starting to look like a boneyard. After several weeks, the paleontologists have uncovered many fossils. Just a few feet away, Pat is digging out part of a crocodile skull, while Kristi Curry, one of Cathy's students, is working on a titanosaur leg bone that's almost as big as she is. Titanosaurs belong to the sauropod group, the largest of all dinosaurs. They have long necks and tails and an elephantlike body.

At the other end of the scale, Dave has just found a tiny vertebra from a snake's backbone. "Hey, I found another sand treasure," he says, carefully putting it in a small jar and placing it with a row of other jars containing tiny fish bones, pieces of turtle, and other small fossils. "The amazing thing about this quarry," Dave explains, "is that you never know what's going to turn up. There are many different animals here."

That's because the rock at the quarry belongs to the Late Cretaceous period, about 70 million years ago, that had a great diversity of life. At that time, dinosaurs were king but they shared the land with frogs, snakes, turtles, and crocodiles, as well as primitive mammals and birds—the ancestors of the animals we are familiar with today.

The other exciting thing about the quarry is that almost all of the discoveries are new to science. Nearly everything known about dinosaurs is based on fossils from the northern continents, especially North America

Opposite: A bone from the mystery animal is carefully examined.

Below: A theropod tooth.

Above: Numerous bones have been excavated at the quarry. In the foreground, a large sauropod dinosaur bone has been covered with a protective plaster jacket.

Opposite: Cathy digs around the bones of the animal that Dave found in the quarry.

and Europe. The southern areas such as Africa, South America, and Madagascar have their own important stories to tell, and scientists are only now starting to unearth them.

One such discovery was made in 1996, when the team dug out one of the best-preserved theropod skulls ever found. A skull is highly prized for the information it contains. For example, paleontologists can tell what sort of food the animal ate by examining its teeth. They can tell how big its brain was from the size of the brain case. They can also identify the species, which in this case was one that had only been known from a few tiny bone fragments. With such a good specimen the paleontologists could properly describe the animal for the first time. It was a spectacular predator almost thirty feet long, with a curious horn in the middle of its forehead. Strangest of all, it resembled a theropod discovered in Argentina. This was very important, because it showed that the southern continents were once closer together and that dinosaurs could cross between Madagascar and South America on dry land.

Cathy looks out across the sunburnt hills, trying to imagine how the landscape appeared when dinosaurs roamed the area. Nobody really knows, but Ray Rogers, the team geologist, has been studying the rocks. "You can see how this layer of sandstone we are digging is several feet thick," he says. "An ancient flood laid this down, so we know the quarry was once a riverbed. In fact this region was probably part of a large coastal plain crossed by several rivers on their way to the sea, much as it is today."

Ray's explanation makes it easier to picture the ancient scene. Crocodiles sunbathed by the banks of these rivers, while primitive birds and mammals found refuge in patches of woodland. Marshes and small swampy pools were filled with fish and frogs. And of course there were dinosaurs. It must have been a breathtaking sight, as long-necked sauropods grazed the shrubs and fierce theropods hunted the smaller animals.

"The climate then was most likely seasonal," Ray continues, "with long dry periods followed by sudden heavy rains. So it's not hard to imagine some dinosaurs getting trapped by rising floodwaters during a really massive storm, then being washed into the river and drowned. Others, already dead, may have been lying close to the riverbank. Their bodies would have been swept downstream and washed up on sandbars, where they were soon buried by more sand washed down by the flood. That's what we are digging up here—the buried victims of just such a storm!"

Luckily for the paleontologists, that's the perfect situation for fossil formation. When a freshly killed dinosaur is buried quickly, its bones are not left on the surface to rot or be broken up and scattered by other animals. In fact, most of the bones from the quarry are so perfectly preserved the animals appear to have died only a few months ago, not 70 million years ago. Under a microscope the paleontologists can see fine details, like the tiny channels where nerves and blood capillaries once penetrated the bone. They can even get some idea of how old each dinosaur was when it died.

But there is one drawback to the quarry. Because the dinosaurs were washed downstream in a flood, their bones are sometimes jumbled up. The quarry is like a huge fossil jigsaw puzzle with some of the pieces missing. The paleontologists often have to work out which leg goes with which arm, and so on!

Prospecting for a New Quarry

At breakfast, Cathy and Kristi decide to spend the day looking for a new quarry site. After six weeks in the field, the team has uncovered most of the fossils at the old quarry. "We call this prospecting," Cathy says, "and we do it by walking around and looking for loose bones lying on the ground. When we find some, we search uphill to check the sandstone layer they weathered out of. And if we see more bones buried in the sandstone, that's where we dig!"

As they hike across the landscape, it's not hard to find fossils. Everywhere, small pieces of ancient turtle shell litter the ground like broken pottery. "This must have been turtle heaven at one time," Cathy remarks. "If we saw a large piece we would take it, but these bits of shell are of no interest."

Then Cathy suddenly picks up a tiny fossil fragment, which her experienced eye recognizes as part of a frog skull. It's a good sign that the spot was once close to a stream or swamp, so she decides to do some surface collecting for other fossils.

Surface collecting means lying flat on your belly and searching the ground as if you've dropped a pin on the floor. It's slow work, but it's the only way to find tiny fossils. And as Cathy explains, the small fossils are often as important as the big ones. "For instance, this fossil frog is unlike any of the frogs that live in Madagascar now. So this poses some questions. Why did it become extinct, and where did the modern frogs come from?

"Answering these questions can lead us in new directions. We know that the modern-day frogs could not have swum to the island of Madagascar, because frogs die in salt water. So perhaps they got here on floating rafts of trees and plants. Sometimes a really big flood will sweep pieces of forest far out to sea, like floating islands that carry animals with them. This might be one way the frogs got here. Perhaps it's also how some other modern-day animals like lemurs reached Madagascar. A small fossil like this can be a very big clue to understanding the past!"

As she crawls over the ground, Cathy sometimes scoops up loose sandy rock and sieves it for tiny fossils. Soon she is satisfied with a collection of fish bones and scales, which she places in a small jar. Next she gives the site its own identification number, which she records in her notebook. Every location where a fossil is collected gets a number. This one is Mad 98-29, which means that it's the twenty-ninth fossil site searched during the 1998 Madagascar expedition.

Then she reaches into her backpack for an instrument called a Global Positioning System, or GPS. When the GPS is on, it receives radio information from several satellites in orbit above the earth, giving the site's exact position in latitude and longitude. Cathy copies down the reading:

Opposite: With a pickax over one shoulder, Cathy sets off with Kristi to look for a new quarry site. *Below:* The ground is littered with thousands of fossil fragments, many of which are ancient turtle shell.

Below: The loose sandy rock is sieved for small fossils, such as fish bones and mammal teeth.
Right: Cathy discovers a fossil frog bone at the Mad 98-29 site.

"south 15°53'49. 7" east 46°34'45. 0"." With this record of where the fossils were found, she can easily return to the same location.

Cathy and Kristi climb in and out of gullies and over small hills looking for fossil remains. Although the land seems barren, there are small surprises for the watchful. A crimson dragonfly perches like a jewel on the pale yellow grass. A chameleon stares back at them from the bushes with swiveling eyes. Often they spot hawks soaring in the perfect blue sky, hunting for small game.

Occasionally they pick up a small fossil lying on the ground—a daggerlike tooth from a theropod or a fragment of rib—but these are isolated findings and do not indicate a large fossil bed nearby. Then, after a couple of hours, as they round a gentle slope, Kristi spots two sauropod vertebrae on the ground. Looking a few feet uphill, she discovers part of another bone poking out of the sandstone.

Cathy decides it's worth digging a test trench into the hill to see if there are more buried fossils. They take turns swinging the pickax, loosening and digging away the soil above the fossil-bearing sandstone. Then they pick at the fossil layer more carefully with their awls. "Looks like a sauropod shoulder blade," Kristi calls excitedly as she unearths part of it. "And I can see other stuff here too. I think we might have a quarry site."

But they do not dig any further. Cathy decides to leave this quarry for next season. With only a week left in this year's expedition, there are not enough days to excavate it properly. She covers up the trench with loose earth and records the site location with her GPS.

Left: The location of Mad 98-29 is pinpointed using the Global Positioning System.

Above: Cathy swings the pickax to open up a new quarry site.

Burlap
and Plaster

It's 7:30 A.M., and the team is loading the pickup truck with bags of plaster, piles of burlap sacks, buckets, and large water drums. With a loud thump, Dave hoists aboard the last fifty-pound bag of plaster. "Today we're going to get ready to move the fossils out of the quarry," he says. "First we have to jacket them with plaster so they can be lifted safely and shipped home."

As soon as the materials are hauled into the quarry, the team splits up. Some people start cutting the burlap into long four-inch-wide strips. Others dig a trench around the base of each fossil so that it stands on a pedestal of sandstone. Cathy pulls out a long measuring tape and starts mapping the fossils with Kristi. "Before any fossil is moved from the quarry, we draw a map showing the exact position where it was found," Cathy says. "This will help us back in the lab, when we are trying to figure out which bone goes with which."

Once the bones are mapped, Dave and Scott begin the jacketing. Plaster is poured into a bucket of water and mixed to the right consistency. Some tissue paper is put on each bone so that the plaster will not stick to it. Then Scott dips strips of burlap into the wet plaster and hands them to Dave, who lays them on the fossil, gently pressing and molding each one to the shape of the bone. The tighter the jacket fits around the bone, the better it is protected. Layer by layer, Dave swaddles the fossil like a well-bandaged mummy.

By midafternoon the quarry looks like a field of giant mushrooms. Each fossil wears a white cap of plaster, dried into a hard protective shell. Now the team begins the next step. They use their

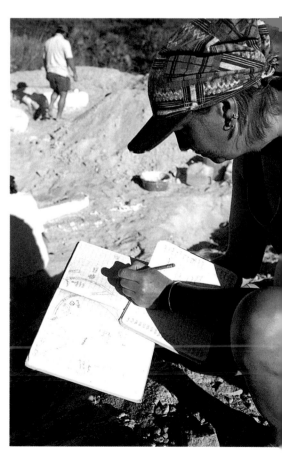

Opposite: Scott dips each burlap strip into the plaster mix and hands it to Dave who wraps it around the fossil. *This page:* Before any fossil is removed from the quarry, its position is carefully measured and mapped.

Below: Plaster-soaked burlap is molded around the fossils.
Right: Carrying poles are attached to the largest fossils.
Opposite: The school celebration.

awls to chip at the sandstone pedestal beneath each fossil. Once the fossil is free, they carefully flip it over and quickly cover its underside with more plaster strips.

It's almost sunset by the time they get to the last fossil, a huge femur from the leg of a titanosaur. It takes five people just to flip it over. The others wonder how they are going to haul the monster bone out, but Dave has a plan. Later that evening he will ask the villagers if they can help the next day.

The School Celebration

The team members take turns going into Mahajanga for supplies, and today it is Cathy and Ray's job. But it's no chore: market day in Mahajanga is like a carnival. Ancient taxis and brightly painted *pousse-pousses* (rick-shaws) share the narrow streets with creaky carts, hauled by large hump-backed cattle called zebu.

The market itself is a maze of small alleyways, where traders are selling everything from chickens to china teapots. Cathy ducks and weaves between stalls piled with woven baskets and straw hats. She looks at exquisite carvings, strings of beads, polished gemstones, and tablecloths embroidered in rainbow col-ors. Nearby, piles of dried fish gleam like

silver coins next to bundles of spices—nutmeg, saffron and cloves—arranged in tidy rows. There are sticky black pods of the vanilla orchid, unusual-looking fruits, and freshly washed vegetables heaped in large glistening mounds.

As she checks off the shopping list, Cathy's baskets fill with tangerines, rice, tomatoes, pineapples, beans, bananas, and lentils. She's thankful that Ray is there to help. Today extra supplies are needed because the villagers are preparing a feast to share with the paleontologists in celebration of the building of the frame for the schoolhouse. Eventually everything is loaded aboard the pickup truck, which strains under the weight as it heads back across the dusty plains to Berivotra.

After Cathy delivers the party supplies to the village, she goes to the quarry to help the others, who have been busy carrying out the fossils. It's hard work in the afternoon sun, and everyone has to watch their footing on the rough track between the quarry and the road. Some of the young men from the village have turned up to help carry the biggest plaster jackets. They know the terrain and carry the bones with an easy grace.

Finally it's time to haul out the large sauropod femur. The young men debate among themselves for a long time, deciding on the best way to carry it. They lash it to sturdy wooden poles, and then eight of the strongest men hoist it onto their shoulders in a single movement. Their faces crease in concentration and their knees buckle with the weight as they slowly

Opposite: Cathy ducks between stalls at the Mahajanga market.

Below, left: Pousse-pousse is a great way to get around the city.

Below, right: Cathy hauls out a sauropod rib bone.

move off down the track.

To keep his helpers in step, the leader sings a Malagasy chant that means "we don't work with weak men." The others think this is hilarious and join in, getting louder and more boisterous as they approach the road, where with a loud cheer they lift the huge bone onto the truck.

Back in the village, the women have been busy preparing vegetables and filling huge pots with rice and stewed zebu for the feast. Smoke and cooking smells filter into the evening air and young children play near the adults. As soon as everyone arrives, the celebration begins. The children perform special dances, and the women sing. Then an elder offers a solemn prayer of thanks.

The people gather around the open walls of the half-built schoolhouse as the food is passed out. Then Dave shares the news that he will organize a charitable foundation to help the school. The parents smile openly to hear that the children will be able to have an education. The paleontologists are thankful, too, that they are able to return some of the kindness shown to them.

The team is also happy to have completed another successful expedition. Soon Cathy and the others will leave Madagascar until the next year's expedition. The fossils will be wrapped in straw and packed in wooden crates for their long journey to America. After the paleontologists have finished studying the fossils, they will be returned to the people of Madagascar and kept in a museum in the capital city of Antananarivo.

Below, left: Large cooking pots are filled with rice for the feast.

Below, right: Everyone sits around the walls of the half-built schoolhouse as the food is served.

Putting the Clues Together

Back in her university office, Cathy gets a phone call: twelve large crates are waiting at the docks in New York City. She hires a small truck to collect the fossils and clear them through Customs. It's a moment of excitement and apprehension. Has the precious cargo survived its two-month journey across the sea?

Everyone crowds around the crates as they are opened back at the university. There's a sigh of relief when they see that the fossils seem to be in good condition. The fossil crocodile and sauropod bones will be forwarded to the other paleontologists who joined the expedition, while the smaller, birdlike fossils will be kept for study.

Now the final stage of the process begins. The plaster jackets are cut away and the fossils cleaned of all remaining sandstone by the preparator, Virginia Heisey. Preparing fossils for study is a very skilled job. Virginia works with the same tools a dentist uses—probes, picks, brushes, and small drills. A single bone takes hours to prepare and coat with glue for protection, while a large sandstone block may keep her busy for weeks. Often she works under a microscope to free the smallest fragments, laying aside each chip so that they may be reassembled into complete bones. It takes extraordinary patience, but Virginia has plenty of that; when she isn't preparing fossils she works as a school bus driver!

One by one, the jackets that may contain bird bones are opened and prepared. When Cathy examines the fossils more closely, she finds that some are from a small theropod dinosaur. Another turns out to be the leg bone of a frog. But she also discovers several tiny bird bones, including a wing bone from an animal that is new to science.

Even though only a few bird bones are eventually uncovered, Cathy is not discouraged. "There are never any guarantees about what you will find," she says, "especially when you are looking for such small, thin-walled bones. It's exciting just to have found this much bird material. Some of these fossil fragments will add valuable information about the types of birds that lived alongside the dinosaurs."

You need perseverance to be a good paleontologist. "If you have that," Cathy says, "then occasionally you might be lucky enough to make a really big discovery." That was what happened in 1995, when the team found the bones of a small animal buried in the quarry in Madagascar. Cathy thought one of the bones was from a wing, but there was no way to be sure. The team dug out the whole animal, still encased in a yard-long block of sandstone, and shipped it back to the university.

Opposite: The sickle claw from the primitive bird *Rahonavis* proved to be a spectacular missing link. *Below:* Once each jacket is opened, Virginia begins the painstaking task of freeing the fossil bones from the sandstone.

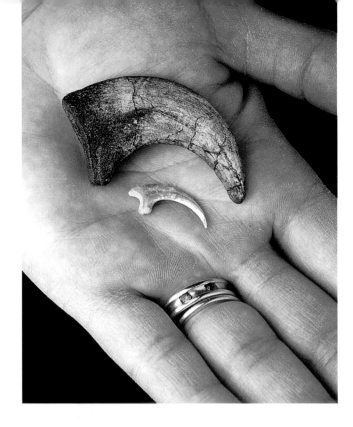

As soon as Virginia had freed the "wing" bone at the lab, Cathy examined it. With the help of a microscope she confirmed her suspicions. Along the length of the bone were tiny knobs where feathers were once attached. Next, Virginia discovered something even more exciting—a long, bony reptilian tail. This meant that the bird was very primitive, with features of both bird and dinosaur.

The biggest surprise came last. While Virginia started preparing the foot, Cathy joked that it would be funny if the bird had a sickle claw. She was thinking how birds are thought to be related to a group of theropod dinosaurs that had special hooked claws to disembowel their prey, as *Velociraptor* did. Later that day, as Cathy was teaching a class of students, the news broke. Dave called her from the lab to say that Virginia had found a sickle claw! This was an important discovery—a primitive bird with a sickle claw. No one had ever found anything like it before.

In the end, Virginia found bones from the bird's legs, feet, arm, back, tail, hip, and shoulder—enough to give Cathy some very important information. She measured many features of these bones—the number of toes, whether some bones were fused together, the shape of the hip bones and so on—and used a computer to compare these with the same features from several other birds and dinosaurs. This process is called "cladistics," a method scientists use to work out a family tree showing how different animals are related. The more features two animals share, the more closely they are likely to be related.

What animal was closest to Cathy's bird? The answer the computer gave was a great surprise—*Archaeopteryx*. She had found the closest known relative of the famous *Archaeopteryx*, discovered more than a hundred years earlier. The computer also told her that the fossil shared many features with theropod dinosaurs, especially the unusual sickle claw. The sickle claw was a spectacular missing link—helping to prove that birds *are* related to dinosaurs.

Below: The reconstruction of *Rahonavis. Opposite:* Cathy visits the American Museum of Natural History in New York to discuss her discoveries.

There was one more thing that Cathy wanted to know. What did this bird look like? She asked an artist at the university, Luci Betti-Nash, to draw a reconstruction. With so few bones to go on, it wasn't easy to do. Luci relied on drawings of *Archaeopteryx* to fill in the missing parts and bring the fossil back to life. What she drew was a fearsome bird the size of a hawk, with a large sickle claw on each foot. Cathy called it *Rahonavis,* from the Malagasy word *rahona,* which means a cloud or menace, and the Latin word *avis,* which means bird. She thought it was a good name for an airborne predator.

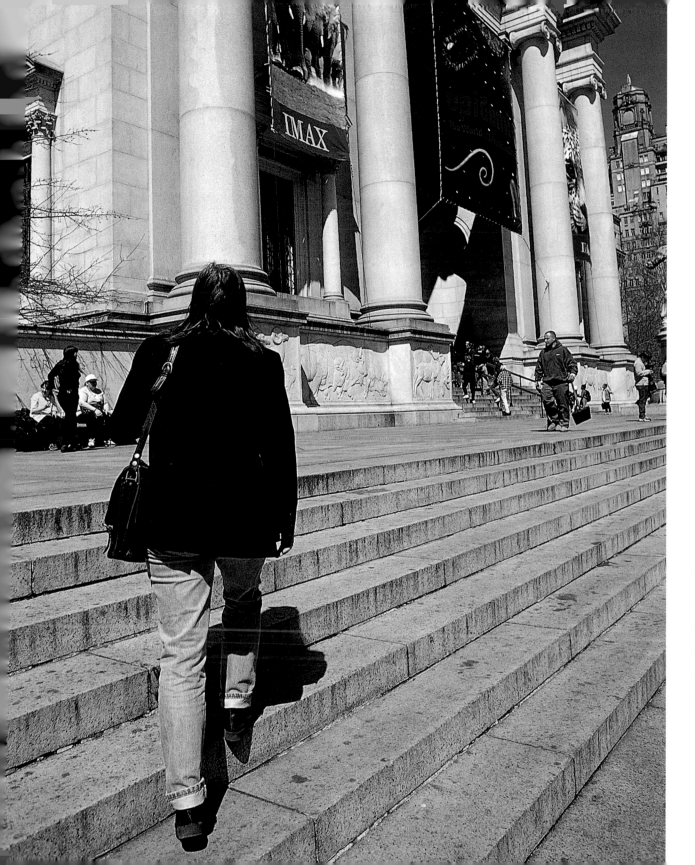

The Museum

Cathy pauses at the entrance to the American Museum of Natural History in New York, recalling her excitement as a little girl visiting her favorite *Triceratops*. This time she is bringing her own findings. She has come to talk with a fellow paleontologist, Luis Chiappe, about the fossils she has brought back from Madagascar.

Luis has recently returned from his own expedition, so the two have much to discuss. He tells her of his discovery in South America of a huge titanosaur nesting site. He found thousands of fossil eggs littering the ground, some so perfectly preserved they still had the remains of baby dinosaurs inside. Then Cathy talks about her findings in Madagascar.

She opens a box containing the

few delicate bones that Virginia has prepared. They examine each one carefully, trying to identify it and figure out what bird it came from. Was it a large bird or a small one? Are the bones from a primitive bird-dinosaur or do they more closely resemble those of modern birds?

Like Cathy, Luis has studied fossil birds for many years, so the opportunity to discuss these questions is valuable for both of them. Sharing knowledge helps scientists clarify the strengths and weaknesses of their ideas. It helps them see the importance of their findings more clearly and understand what they must do next.

Cathy knows there is plenty more to be done. Even though paleontologists have been collecting for over a hundred years, you could still fit all of the world's fossil bird discoveries into a room the size of a small bedroom. Her work in Madagascar has added to our understanding, but it will be decades more before the mysteries of bird evolution are truly revealed.

For Cathy, that's reassuring. She loves nothing better than digging for clues that make sense of our planet's ancient history. As she walks down the museum steps, she is already thinking about next year's expedition to Madagascar.

postscript

What happened to the other fossils brought back from the 1998 expedition? Cathy reports that the paleontologists are still preparing them, but there are already some exciting finds. "We think the sauropod bones belong to a new species of dinosaur, and what is really exciting is that we also have some of the animal's skull, which may give us useful information about its owner." A sauropod skull is a very rare find, probably because it is so much smaller and more delicate than the rest of the dinosaur.

Perhaps the most unusual discovery so far is a pug-nosed crocodile. "It's a really weird-looking creature," Cathy says, "since it doesn't have a snout like a modern crocodile. The only other fossil crocodile that looks anything like it was discovered in South America, so once again that's important evidence that South America and Madagascar were once much closer together, and that animals could cross between them."

acknowledgments

I wish to thank Cathy Forster for her unfailing patience throughout the production of this book, and Dave Krause, who organized the Madagascar expedition and kindly allowed me to join it. Thanks, too, to Vivien for putting up with my absence and for putting me back on my feet after I returned.

For help with editing, I am grateful to my mother, Audrey, and my excellent editor, Amy Flynn. For planting the seed of this book, thank you, Anita Silvey.

To all the team members of the expedition—your good company and patient instruction in paleontology are appreciated.

For making my visit to Madagascar a memorable chapter in my own life, I would like to thank the warm-natured people of Berivotra and especially all their wonderfully considerate, joyfully eager, and eternally smiling children.

A Missing Link

Can you spot some ways in which *Rahonavis* was part bird and part dinosaur? It had sickle claws and a long bony tail like *Velociraptor*, and probably had teeth and three clawed fingers on each hand. These features are lost or reduced in modern birds. The pigeon has no teeth and its tail is a stump, while some of its fingers are fused together as part of the wing. But the breastbone, to which powerful flight muscles are attached, has become enormous. These changes have made modern birds lighter and improved their ability to fly.

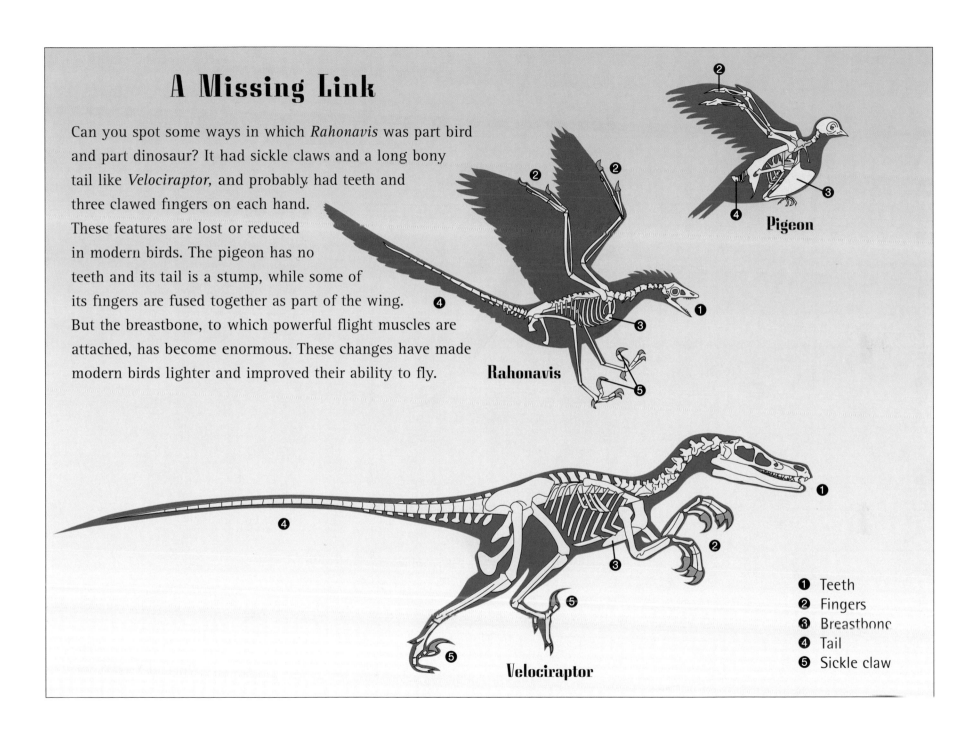

Pigeon

Rahonavis

Velociraptor

❶ Teeth
❷ Fingers
❸ Breastbone
❹ Tail
❺ Sickle claw

further reading

Searching for Velociraptor, by Lowell Dingus and Mark A. Norell (New York: Harper Collins, 1996), tells of the discovery of a fossil *Velociraptor* in the Gobi Desert. Two paleontologists describe how the dinosaur was found and how it was prepared for study.

Tracking Dinosaurs in the Gobi, by Margery Facklam (New York: Twenty-First Century, 1997), is an account of the American Museum of Natural History's expeditions, past and present, to the Gobi Desert of Mongolia.

Dinosaur Dig, by Kathryn Lasky (New York: Morrow, 1990), is about a family that joins a dinosaur dig in Montana.

New Dinosaurs: Skeletons in the Sand, by Elaine Pascoe (Woodbridge, Conn.: Blackbirch Press, 1998), describes a dinosaur expedition to the Sahara Desert of Africa.

The Puzzle of the Dinosaur-Bird, by Miriam Schlein (New York: Dial, 1996), provides a wonderful account of the discovery of *Archaeopteryx* and the scientific debate over birds and dinosaurs.

help
berivotra school

Dave Krause is asking for donations to provide a teacher and school supplies for the children of Berivotra. If you wish to help, please send a check to:

The Madagascar Ankizy Fund
The Stony Brook Foundation (account no. 284300)
State University of New York
Stony Brook, NY 11794-1188

index